Inspiring Library Stories
Tales of Kindness, Connection, and Community Impact

Edited, and with essays, by Oleg Kagan

HINCHAS
Press

HINCHAS Press

Los Angeles, California

Library of Congress Cataloging-in-Publication Data
Oleg Kagan
Inspiring Library Stories: Tales of Kindness, Connection, and Community
Impact
ISBN 978-1-7324848-6-3
Library of Congress Control Number: 2020918162

Editor: Oleg Kagan
Cover Design: Autumn Anglin, www.greygirlgraphics.com
Interior Book Design: Autumn Anglin
Illustrations: Autumn Anglin

Published by
(cc) 2020 HINCHAS Press
Los Angeles, California 90066
www.hinchaspress.com

Book Printing Stats: DIN Condensed Bold, Garamond Premier Pro
Printed and bound by: KDP

Printed in the United States of America.

ISBN 978-1-7324848-6-3

This book is dedicated to all of the yea-saying library workers who serve their communities with kindness and dedication. Never underestimate your power to change lives.

A portion of the proceeds from this book are being donated to EveryLibrary, a non-partisan, pro-library organization whose mission is to help "...public, school, and college libraries win bonding, tax, and advisory referendum, ensuring stable funding and access to libraries for generations to come." More information about EveryLibrary can be found at everylibrary.org.

CONTENTS

FOREWORD

By Yago Cura

> "The greatest part of a writer's time is spent in reading, in order to write: a man will turn over half a library to make one book."
>
> —Samuel Johnson

I don't know where I first met Oleg; it doesn't matter where I first met Oleg. I know he is a courageous soul, well-enough-courageous to collaborate with someone like me. It's not that I am overtly annoying or spectacularly pernicious (I am sure some of you disagree); it's that deep down inside, Oleg and I should find the utility of being rivals more useful?

I know Oleg because we do a similar job but for different-not-different masters. I also know Oleg because our baby sons play together on Friday mornings at a local airport park. The point is that even though we work for competing organizations, I don't think we've ever felt the necessity to unnecessarily compete with each other. I think we both feel very fortunate to ply our trade under the same sun, despite the origins of the shadows we might cast. Oleg and I are loyal and ambitious, but we try not to let the little things perturb our planetary alignments (wife + kids).

I once gave a presentation to an auditorium full of Oleg's colleagues, and it wasn't until I was able to catch up with him during the intermission that I felt that my presentation had been a small bit successful. Another time, Oleg came to the West LA Regional Branch, enemy territory, to attend a monthly zine workshop I was faciliating with Adult Librarian, Carrie Davies. Carrie and I were garnering 20-25 people a month at our workshops until the pandemic body slammed our best efforts (year-long schedule of facilitators) in what has been the cage match we are calling 2020. These two moments serve as births for this endeavor—supporting Oleg and Autumn, the intrepid artist/book designer, behind *Inspiring Library Stories: Tales of Kindness, Connection, and Community Impact.*

While Oleg made a zine detailing his son's birth story, he told me about the work he had already done incubating what you hold in your hand: Inspiring Library Stories. I listened intently because for the past three years I have been publishing the *Librarians with Spines* series with Max Macias and Autumn Anglin. I instantly thought of Autumn because I knew that without Autumn, Max and I could not have completed even the first volume of *Librarians with Spines*. It's not that Autumn is partners with Max and I; it is that when we Voltron into our book-making triumvirate—we move effortlessly to make books transpire. That doesn't mean the books are excellent or that the content will be up to your particular standards, but if you've ever had to make a book, you can attest to the importance of knowing how to heave.

Please enjoy the book you hold in your hand, and please help us to get one of these into every library in the U.S., so we can continue to provide residents of the U.S. with stellar library resources and services. At least 30% of the proceeds of this book are going directly to EveryLibrary (https://www.everylibrary.org/) as a straight, quarterly donation. Oleg and HINCHAS Press are splitting the rest in the hopes of selling enough books to buy one of those old studio houses on the hill in Mar Vista that overlooks LMU, Palms, and Westwood, and glimmering slip of the beach at Venice.

INTRODUCTION

During my first librarian job up at the Lancaster Library in California's Antelope Valley, I had many regular patrons. One was a student at a large university in Los Angeles, over an hour's drive from her home. Since mine was the biggest library in the area, that's where she came to do some of the research for her Master's program. Over my year and a half there, I found books and articles for her, helped her structure big ideas in her papers, and pepped her up when she felt discouraged. After she turned in her final thesis paper, I remember her coming to the reference desk looking relieved and joyful.

"I couldn't have done it without you," she said, smiling. I won't lie, it felt good to have been part of her achievement. Still, I didn't feel like I had done anything truly special; after all, helping people is what librarians do, isn't it? So unremarkable was this occasion that I mentioned it to my girlfriend at the time (now my wife) and promptly forgot about it until putting together this book.

I first had the idea for a book of library impact stories, or short anecdotes showing the positive influence of librarians or library workers on patrons, in 2015. On a whim, I made a post asking for stories at the largest library-related group on Facebook (hello, ~~ALA~~Library Think Tank!). Unsurprisingly, many people responded, and a few even sent me stories! But like many good ideas, this one took a back seat to other projects. In 2017, it got something of a revival when I was invited to speak about library impact stories, among other topics, at the CLA/ Califa Yosemite Institute for Small and Rural Libraries. A few participants of that gathering also contributed stories. During the same year, I served as the Founding Editor of EveryLibrary's *Medium Magazine*, a position which gave me the opportunity to advocate for libraries through weekly articles (a few of which became the essays in this book), and help other writers do the same. It was only at the beginning of this year, 2020, after a fruitful conversation with outreach librarian-extraordinaire and publisher, Yago Cura, owner of HINCHAS Press, that this project got its third wind.

While a lot has happened in the world during these five years, the landscape for communicating about libraries has changed little. Library advocates cite impressive statistics about the billions of visits libraries get every year, or how there are more libraries in the United States then there are Starbucks, or that one Neil Gaiman nugget: "Google can bring you back 100,000 answers. A librarian can bring you back the right one." And it's true. Libraries are popular; more than half of the people in the United States have library cards, and many have visited at least once in the past year. Moreover, they're a wise financial choice for communities; return-on-investment (ROI) studies from all over the country show that, on average, libraries return five dollars for every one dollar spent on them. There's no arguing that libraries put up good numbers, so then why aren't they rewarded with budgets that reflect their obvious benefits? Why is every vote for even a minuscule tax increase a battle? Why don't more decision-makers and community stakeholders understand the importance of libraries?

There is no easy answer here. Likely, it is a combination of many factors, the sum of which could form a whole book in itself, but I'll summarize a few of my opinions on the topic:

- First of all, the narratives about libraries and librarians in our society are riding on at least a century of momentum; misconceptions that libraries are mainly buildings with books, that librarians are stern or mousy gate-keepers, that the whole institution is hopelessly backward technologically have been floating around for decades. They still aren't true.

- Second, there is a culture of fear guiding an anti-library crusade led by tax fundamentalists and prudish control freaks who would sooner rip the first amendment out of the Constitution than allow total strangers free access to information.

- Third, library workers tend not to be boosters by nature. As a group, they are as passionate about their work as they are self-effacing. Part of it, I think, is that librarians tend to become desensitized to the impact of their work – when you spend most of your day helping people, it doesn't seem like such a notable achievement (remember my story above?). This modesty undercuts both everyday advocacy and the big stuff, like when it's time to demonstrate the value of libraries for the City Council during budget time.

This book won't halt society's 100-year old misconceptions about libraries or convince irrational culture warriors to understand freedom of speech, but it will give library lovers some answers when asked the ever-present question: Why should libraries exist?

There are 43 stories here that answer that question from a variety of angles. And it should be noted that while each of these stories are special, they are not unique. Library workers help people find jobs, deal with challenging life events like death, put in extra effort to find answers, show patience in the face of someone's difficult day, provide unexpected kindnesses big and small, and much more. They do it on a daily basis in libraries all over the world and rarely tell anyone about it. Why do they do these things that will never show up in a performance evaluation nor cause them to get a pay bonus or a raise? Why go beyond the pale to assist someone they'll likely never see again? I couldn't tell you why each contributor to *Inspiring Library Stories* acted as they did – to me, their impact overshadows their motives.

That is why this book exists, because despite all of the lovely library statistics, the meaning of this impact is notoriously difficult to quantify. To wit, here we have 43 stories. It's not a big number when you consider that a medium-sized branch library might get 500 visitors a day. Yet, imagine that all of the story's subjects were in the same room as you, and one by one they got onto the microphone and explained how their life was affected by the actions of someone in this book. You would hear from the older woman with difficulty hearing who could enjoy a movie thanks to the library ("Friday Flicks"), or Mr. Uwe Keilitz who learned to read as an adult and is now helping others do the same ("Learning Out Loud"), or the mother of the autistic child who didn't interact with other kids until he participated in a video game tournament at the library ("A Win with Gaming"). Then you would hear forty more stories.

Now, back at our medium-sized branch library, each of those 500 visitors had a reason for coming to the library that day. But let's not get ahead of ourselves. Most of the reasons were simple: To perform research for homework or life, to check out a book, movie, or music for learning or entertainment, to have a quiet environment to work, to take the kids to a science program or concert, to get access to the internet. Fine, and then say, 100 of those visitors needed something more particular. Maybe 50 of them had a problem only a librarian could solve, and 10 of those were special like the examples in this book. According to the American Library Association, there were 16,568 public library buildings in the United States in 2016. Not all of them were medium-sized branches, but you get the point. A little multiplication and it's obvious that there are a lot of untold library stories out there! It's not so far-fetched, is it?

It certainly isn't a stretch for me since I was one of those stories. I talk about Hannah Kramer later on in the essay "The Important Emotional Labor of Librarians That Most People Never Think About" – she was the Senior Librarian at the Will & Ariel Durant Library, the library of my youth. When you're a kid, not too many adults pay attention to you, but Hannah paid attention to me and my brother. As did the other staff at the library; they treated us with respect then, and later when we volunteered at the library, they made us feel like we were part of the family. When I got hired and actually became part of the staff, I discovered that this wasn't special, it was just how they normally treated people.

You see, my story isn't one clear-cut event, it's a string of generosity. So, when it came time in my education to decide what I wanted to be, I thought back to my youth when I wanted to pitch a tent in the library, and then my teenage years when Hannah let me and my brother help read to elementary school kids during a visit. Or to a few years later, when clarinet aficionado (and young adult librarian) Al Rice let me teach poetry to visiting high-schoolers. I thought about these opportunities to serve, and wanted nothing more than to do that every day. I became a librarian.

Are you surprised that I love libraries? If I could bottle up this feeling and sell it (or give it away—why not?), I would. But I can't, so I did the next best thing and teamed up with forty-something collaborators to put it in a book. Be careful reading on. The stories in this book have power. They could make you laugh or cry, or both. Either way, my hope is that they inspire or affirm a belief that libraries are essential to our lives, now and forever.

Oleg Kagan
July 2nd, 2020
Los Angeles, California, USA

BOOKS & READING

The strongest association people traditionally have with libraries is the subject of the chapter that starts us off. Here we see the wonderful aura reading provides, how easy it is to forget that free and unrestricted libraries are a unique and special concept, and that gaining literacy is wonderful at any age.

THE MAGIC OF READING

Imagine a room with ten children ranging in ages from seven to twelve. They are all highly-intelligent, focused, and simply delightful. We are all meeting for my Cool Kids Reading Club and discussing the The Sixty-Eight Rooms by Marianne Malone.

I read the first chapter of the book. The first chapter is twelve pages long with 12-point font without illustrations. I expect the children to get restless and bored. But they are all in rapt attention; they like to hear me read. But I'm still shy. I recall being self-conscious of reading when I was learning English. I recall stuttering and being laughed at. But I sit and take my time and read. I change my voice to sound out the characters of the main girl Ruthie, her best friend Jack, and the other characters.

The setting of the book is the Thorne Rooms at the Chicago Art Institute. These are sixty-eight miniatures of actual historical rooms. Some kids have not read the book, and I summarize that the characters in the book find a magic key that allows them to shrink and enter the miniature rooms, once inside they open real doors and windows into different historical time periods. They are enthralled and their imaginations begin to blossom.

I ask: If you were a time traveler, what time period would you choose? I tell the children, for me it's the

1920s and how comfortable I feel looking at buildings, clothes, and photographs from that time.

"If I was a time traveler, I would travel back to 2006." says Lucy.

"That's not that far, is that the year you were born?" Yes, she giggles.

Two boys say "We want to travel into the future."

I reply: Don't worry, you will. All of you will travel into the future and come back to this library and remember the past, this moment when you were children and meeting here.

"Do you want me to continue the chapter?"

"Oh, yes yes. Please read to us!"

Half of the kids get up and gather behind me. I wish somebody had taken a picture. Angelina is leaning over my left shoulder, her cheek is less than an inch away from my cheek. Them watching me read is truly magical and wonderful; one of my favorite life experiences.

Lada W.
Los Angeles, CA

AN INTERNATIONAL PERSPECTIVE

While doing some unofficial community outreach at the 2016 Republican National Convention, a fellow librarian and I had a short, but wonderful, conversation with a passing stranger.

As we were walking a now-empty book bike toward our neighborhood, we met up with a gentleman who seemed a bit lost. He had been given directions downtown that involved a 40-minute walk, when he was standing only a few yards away from an RTA station that would take him directly there.

We walked him back over to the train stop, and on the way, we found out that Reza, a journalist from Orange County, fled Iran with his wife and children 30 years ago. He told us this:

"What you are doing reminds me of my youth, we'd put books on bikes, on donkeys, on whatever we had..."

"...the only difference is, we'd get arrested."

Don't ever forget that what librarians do is so awesome that it is illegal in some parts of the world.

Jon
Cleveland, OH

IT ONLY GETS BETTER

Yesterday a 70+ year old man came into the library to get his first library card in celebration of having just learned how to read. He sat in the children's library reading *Hop on Pop* with his tutor and I almost cried, it was so cute.

After he finished the book his tutor said, "See, you're reading just like everyone else in the library!" To which he responded: "This is fun!"

It only gets better, my dude, it only gets better.

Nikki D.
Blount County Public Library

READING TO DEVIN

Devin had an unusual thirst for knowledge. When he started kindergarten his teacher organized a contest. The goal was for someone to read him a book every night, which his mother and father were already doing. At 6, he wasn't as specific about his tastes as his older brother, who was into inventing. He wanted me to read everything to him. As a grandma, my budget was tight and we quickly graduated to the library. I soon realized that having him pick out the books would be a lengthy process, so instead I would go to the library when it opened and check out ten.

When I picked Devin up from school he walked into the house and the books were on the coffee table. "Come on, grandma," he encouraged me, dropping his lunch box and papers on the floor on the way to the couch. His eyes got bigger and he sat down waiting for me, peering over the top of the books smiling. When I finally sat down he cozied up to my side under my arm. He didn't move, watching the pile go down, and was disappointed when it was finished. At that point, I would kiss him on top of his head and promise to get more tomorrow.

I graduated too, with a book cart. Eric, the children's librarian stood up when I came down the stairs to the children's section and helped me load the cart with whole sections of books. We didn't look at the titles and when I checked out with a volunteer, she would often say this is a lost one they'd have been looking for. But I was never disappointed since there were so many others for Devin.

Oh, we won that contest with 2,000 books read and I am sure that Devin, at age 8, remembers each one.

Gail Javadi
Lancaster, CA

CONNECTIONS

Though books and libraries tend to be synonymous in people's minds, libraries are really about connections – whether it's two unlikely patrons, a memorable librarian, or a bit of hope in a bleak place. Sure, libraries connect folks with information, but they are also a place where people connect with other people.

GRUMPY GEORGE

Grumpy George sat in his usual chair at his usual table just to the left of the library entrance. He set up his desktop computer just like he did everyday, put on his headphones, and began playing his first-person shooter war games. George is tall and lean, maybe 70. He walks over from veteran's housing nearby and glares at anyone who even thinks of sitting at "his" table.

This day was no different. No different except that the person bothering him wasn't at all bothered by him. It was a 10-year-old boy.

"What are you playing?" The boy asked. No answer.

"Is that an AK-47?" No answer.

"Get that guy! Get that guy!" The boy points to the screen. George pushes the boy's hand out of the way, moves his backpack onto the chair next to him, and continues playing.

"Can I watch?" The boy takes a seat at the table behind George, turns around in his chair, and watches over George's shoulder.

Over the next few weeks the boy comes everyday, asking question after question about the game until one day, George doesn't put the backpack on the seat next to him. The boy pulls the chair out and sits down as if they've always shared the table. I look up to see the boy wearing George's much-too-big headphones and controlling the keyboard while George smiles and gives him tips on the game.

Now it's a regular sight to see the boy and his mother sitting on either side of George with their own desktop computer which they carry into the library in its original plastic-handled cardboard box. George leans to one side commenting on the boy's war game, then to the other to help the boy's mother with her resume.

Between their visits, he's usually still grumpy.

Hillary Perelyubskiy
Los Angeles, CA

THE KEY THAT KEEPS ON TURNING

Not long before enrolling for Library School at San Jose State in 1979, I wasn't so sure what I wanted to do for a living. At times I'd wanted to be a sportswriter, a poet, or a teacher, or an athlete. But my world completely rotated when I first encountered Myrt, the Branch Librarian for the Turlock Library. I was living in an 80 year-old house surrounded by fruit trees while attending English classes and playing on the basketball team at Stanislaus State.

I have indelible recollections of the enthusiasm

Myrt exuded. She obviously loved helping people and took great joy in the spirit of discovery. It was almost as though she was an usherette at the Pearly Gates who was handing out as many free passes as possible. She even let me photocopy my turgid poetry on the Library's machine.

From my usual spot at a study table, Myrt was unwaveringly friendly and professional in her many dealings with the public. It seemed like she was acquainted with practically everyone in town —and almost every book on the shelves. She also served as a positive role model for me at a time when I really needed one, although I didn't know it back then. Clearly Myrt has exerted a greater impact on my life than all my heroes combined. She's like Steinbeck, Mother Theresa, John Wooden, and Jimmy Stewart all rolled into one. Only more. Lots more.

A couple of years or so later I received my English degree, and started working as a circulation clerk at the Modesto Library. Unexpectedly, Myrt walked in and I awkwardly tried to express my admiration. My approach was undoubtedly clumsy and she understandably kept going, adding that the air was getting pretty thick. I felt like I'd blown my only chance to express my admiration. Within a few months I left to pursue librarianship at San Jose State and lost track of her, although memories returned regularly. Usually I thought of her when I was helping someone at one of the libraries where I worked, including the same Anaheim Library where my odyssey began. But it wasn't until a few years ago after I'd begun as the Nevada County Librarian that a local resident named Rob and his daughter visited the Madelyn Helling Library and relayed the message from his aunt: "Myrt says hello." Instantly, I knew to whom he was referring. After getting her address I wrote a letter to finally inform her of my long-held esteem. I wasn't so sure she'd even remember me, but she replied with a wonderful letter, informing me that her staff used to secretly call me "Steve with a J", a nickname I'd never heard. I've visited her many times and she even consented to be my "adoptive Greek aunt" when I was running low on family members.

By now I've worked more than 45 years in public libraries, and I've known a lot of truly remarkable and unforgettable people, but if it wasn't for Myrt, I probably wouldn't have met any of them.

Steve Fjeldsted
South Pasadena, CA

THE RED-HAIRED LIBRARIAN

One of my earliest library memories recalls a red-haired, fastidious, librarian who was always brooding through the stacks of books on my numerous visits. She wore dull matching sweater-sets and simple brown tweed skirts. She was thin, but far from frail, and had the demeanor of a drill sergeant, marching through the library in her sensible shoes, her eye-glasses chain set bouncing on her bird-like chest. Nothing escaped her icy stare and she was especially spine-chilling when I checked out books; I would see her up close, glasses perched on the end of her nose, as she loomed over my seven-year-old self, and my stack of *Little House on the Prairie*, Ramona the Pest, and the *Saturday Night Fever* soundtrack on vinyl. This was the summer of 1979 after all and disco had finally made it to the library. The Montgomery-Floyd Regional Library was two blocks away from my house, and my parents allowed me to walk those two blocks alone, fully trusting the sleepy college town where we lived. The library was a magical place for a lonely child like me. Even with the mysterious and moody librarian there, I could escape through books and travel the globe. It was a place where I found new friends, and discovered and fed my imagination, even if it happened to be "Night Fever" by the Bee Gees.

Flash forward ten years to 1989, and disco is dead. For a long time, I forgot about the library just two blocks from home and would drive the 12 miles to the new mall to hang out with friends, eat at the food court, see a movie, and spend money at Waldenbooks. It wasn't until years later, after college, and after I was paying my own rent and bills that I remembered the small town library and sadly all the money I could have saved had I simply walked the two blocks from home and checked out those books for free.

Many things have changed, but one thing that has remained constant since 1979 was that town library on Draper Road in Blacksburg, Virginia. My parents sold the house that I grew up in 1999, and around that time, I paid the library a visit. It had been completely remodeled and revamped, public computers were located in what had once been the adult fiction section. The children's section was now located under the big wide windows that used to be the front entrance. The library was full of energy, it was bright and colorful, long gone were the days of the shushing librarian.

I inquired about the red-haired librarian. Did she still work here? Had she retired?

"Yes, oh yes, Ms. Adams, yes, she retired years ago. What an icon. She was so old-school. Librarians are so different now. She was the end of an era."

I was sad to know that she was gone, I would have liked to talk to her, maybe even ask her about those years, told her that I had grown up to become a librarian also. On my visit, I walked to the back of the library trying to place where the children's room had been circa 1979. For a brief moment, in between the rows of books, I caught a quick glimpse of movement out of the corner of my eye. I turned to look, and just like that, there she was, the red-haired librarian, and she winked at me, pulled her glasses down on the tip of her nose, and smiled, and then, poof, she was gone. Pausing for a moment, still not quite sure what I had just seen, I walked toward the exit, and out into the afternoon sun, humming "Night Fever" by the Bee Gees.

Tracy Michelle Hall-Cole
Spanish Fort, AL (by way of Blacksburg, Virginia)

WHAT ARE THE ODDS?

I am a Friend of the Library and volunteer in the bookstore at Lancaster Library in southern California along with Patricia, a very nice, hard working, and diligent volunteer. One day she was sorting the donations that come into the bookstore, and she found a unique brochure from Yankton, South Dakota, where her brother Steven had attended college in the early 70s!

Patricia had also visited it in 1973, to attend prom. Her brother Steven was the only one of eight siblings who attended college. The family was so poor that in order for him to make it to Yankton, they drove him from Los Angeles to Barstow, gave him $5.00, and sent him on his way. He succeeded, and is now a principal of an elementary school in Tivoli, Texas.

The brochure Patricia found was "The Year of 1928 Brochure of Yankton College," and when she saw the the word Yankton, she exclaimed to her colleague: "My brother went there!" Excited, she then sent the brochure to her brother who then forwarded it to his alma mater.

The folks at the college were very happy to receive this as it helped them put faces to names of places and people from long ago. They sent him a kind and heartfelt letter thanking him and his sister for the donation, and enclosed the March 2016 YC newsletter which discussed the donation at length and expressed their gratitude.

What are the odds that an old brochure from South Dakota would be donated to a small library in Lancaster, California, and discovered by someone who not only knew of the college but would take the time to forward it? It was serendipitous that Patricia was the one who found it. A lucky library story, indeed.

By Denise Schipper
Lancaster, CA

FIRST STEP

My name is Jameson Rohrer and I work for Centinela State Prison in Imperial, California. An inmate who is incarcerated there has been coming to my library on a regular basis since I started. The inmate is from the Los Angeles area and said that he had never stepped foot inside a library in even though he had graduated high school.

The first day he came to the library, I could tell he was nervous and wasn't sure what to do. So I asked him what he was looking for, and we browsed the shelves together. I was doing a reference interview [Library speak for asking open-ended questions to determine a patron's need -Ed.] as we were browsing and found that he was really into history. So we found a few books he was interested in and he went on his way.

The next time he came into the library he told me something I hadn't heard from an inmate directly:

"Mr. Rohrer, I just wanted to say thank you for this wonderful prison library you have built. For the first time in my life I am reading books and enjoying them and discussing the contents with other inmates and sharing the love of reading. When I get out I will be getting my first library card."

Of course this made me feel a sense of accomplishment. If I can even get one inmate to enjoy reading then I am doing my job well.

Jameson Rohrer

THE BIGGEST DIFFERENCE

This took place when I worked in Detroit Redford Branch on the NW side. It was not really a bad area, but had a few gangs around that seemed to want to make the library their territory. I don't know if it was just my attitude that I would not allow that behavior, or the fact that I carried keys to a police mini station in the area, but the library was a neutral place. My attitude was that those kids could be better, do better, and had to be good examples to the younger kids in the library. So I put them out when they misbehaved, but gave them a chance again the next day.

I never knew if I had any effect until about 10 years later, after I was transferred to another branch, and then left the system. I was in a college class at a local college getting the few credits needed for my professional teaching certificate when I noticed a guy with gang tattoos that let me know his gang was from around Redford. At the class break, he came over and said, "Ms. LaPrise is that you?"

It turns out that about 6 months after I was transferred, my words that he could be better and make something of his life sank in. He left the gang, got his GED, and was studying to be a secondary school teacher so he could go back to save more kids. He said I was the first adult that expected better of him, believed he could be, and would not accept his stuff.

While I have been responsible for a few kids growing up to be librarians, this is the real reason I miss working in the city. Sometimes it just takes believing in those others have given up on that make the biggest difference.

Anni West LaPrise
Michigan

ESSAY

THE IMPORTANT EMOTIONAL LABOR OF LIBRARIANS THAT MOST PEOPLE NEVER THINK ABOUT

For librarians, as with many other professions, "Other duties as assigned" is code for tasks that are distasteful, off-kilter, or just plain gross.

I'll be blunt: Almost every librarian I know has a story or three about retrieving something odd (think half-eaten food, cigarettes, live animals) from the book drop, cleaning up feces or other bodily concoctions, or finding members of the public doing foul deeds (clipping their nails, bathing naked in the bathroom, masturbating) in the library. But that's not what this essay is about. For librarians, "other duties as assigned" has another meaning, too.

Most people intuitively understand the emotional load taken on by professions like social workers, nurses, 911 operators, and teachers. Rarely, however, do people consider the emotional labor of librarians. Yet, spend a day at the service desk of a busy library and you'll see people on their best and, too often, their worst days. Spend a few months and you'll begin to follow the lives of your repeat visitors—you'll be privy to, and sometimes help them solve, life's hardest problems. Remember, though, you are one person and they are many so don't get too attached. Spend a few years and it becomes increasingly difficult not to become emotionally involved; you are now a member of the community, hearing about and witnessing the tragedies of everyday life, families breaking up, accidents, the decline of your favorite wisecracking old lady, and death. Plenty of death.

There's plenty of good, too, though. You get to see cute three-foot tall 2nd graders grow into furtive gangling young adult giants, seemingly overnight. You hear about (and sometimes get invited to) weddings, bar mitzvahs, and other important life rituals. And throughout all of that, you keep up a running dialogue about books, movies, vacations, life! You feed the curiosity of your community, and if you're around long enough, they come back and tell you about your influence!

There were a few librarians that saw me grow up. I don't know all of their names, but I remember their faces, and recall the joy with which they served. Ours wasn't a large library, it was just a small branch library in a neighborhood. But a child isn't very big either, so I was never at a loss for something to read.

It was Senior Librarian Hannah Kramer that put me on the path to becoming a librarian. She was kind, and paid attention to all of the kids. As I grew into my teenage years, she didn't tell me how to be a yea-saying librarian, she exemplified it every day. Only later did I learn how hard she fought to establish a Russian literature collection for our community of Soviet refugees. It should be noted that Hannah did not read a word of Russian, but like a perceptive librarian, she noticed highly-literate immigrant parents and grandparents bringing their kids to the library and recognized a need. Thanks to Hannah, my father could relax a little after his 12-hour workdays, reading before bed.

In 2004, our little library closed and re-opened as a new, much larger building, on a busy street. There, I watched Hannah treat everyone with compassion—runaways, drug addicts, the homeless, those experiencing mental illness, and more. Every interaction began with kindness, but if people acted foolish, she, a tiny lady, stood up to them for the good of everyone else's library experience. I worked at that library for years, learning from Hannah with every shift. And in the same month in 2010 when Hannah retired, I began a job as a librarian.

Today, I was at the reference desk and a patron told me that it's like she's been asleep for years and it was time that she woke up and started learning about the world. Can you believe my luck? Purely by chance, it was I that was going to help her do it!

Being a librarian is not an easy job, and it's not because we occasionally have to clean up vile messes. It's not easy because, like Business Librarian Steven Assarian explained in his article, "As a Business Librarian, I Help People Find Their Passion," (https://tinyurl.com/BusinessLibrarian) people sometimes come to us at a crossroads. They're afraid of making a mistake that may put their lives in turmoil. Heck, sometimes their lives are already in turmoil. Librarians take on that chaos; we have no choice but to face down the power, joy and suffering both, that people bring into our space. That's the emotional labor of librarianship. It's not something we often talk about to the public, or even that much to each other. But it's real, it's hard, and it's important.

DEATH

While death may be an unexpected turn for a book of inspiring stories, we know that patrons come into the library during the course of their whole lives, including the challenging times. The stories in this chapter share few commonalities, but one that does stand out is the emotional depth required of each contributor.

A SHARED EXPERIENCE

I recently had a touching moment with a patron who was looking for materials that would help her write an obituary. She mentioned she had never done it and wanted to know how to inject some humor into it.

I found her some items and could see in her eyes she was feeling the way I did when I was faced with writing my father's obituary: Overwhelmed and very raw with grief and shock.

After mentioning my experience with how I managed to write my dad's, she told me she'd be writing her mother's. We teared up together. It was like we were family for a second, sharing grief over the same person. A very special moment. Sad, but beautiful.

I love my work.

Stephanie Stoner
Mesa, AZ

GOSPELS FROM HANK WILLIAMS

One day, Grandma came into the library with tears in her eyes. She walked straight to me and asked for my help.

"I need to find the CD with Christian's favorite song on it."

I looked and looked, but we couldn't find it. It was gone! I told her we can order another copy, and she broke down in tears. She said Christian had killed himself two days earlier – jumped off a bridge. His funeral is tomorrow and she wanted to play this song for him. I told her I would keep looking.

I searched all the local places with no luck and finally I went on Amazon. The song was part of a boxed collection. I bought it with my personal account, and called her. I told her I think I found a copy. She said that it was too late but thanked me anyway.

The CDs came, and I wrapped them up and kept the package at the reference desk. The next time she came in, I said I have something for you. She unwrapped it and looked up at me with tears in her eyes.

She said, "Thank you. My favorite memory of Christian is of him listening to this song over and over."

As a librarian, it isn't just about the books, but the connection to the people that matters.

Erica Richardson
Fort Worth, TX

LOST AND FOUND

Several years ago while working in the library I met the parents of a missing man. Our library is located in a small mountain town and the missing man disappeared nearby during a snowstorm. Though the parents were divorced they had made the trip to our community together to participate in the search for their son.

Search and Rescue was unable to find their son but they spoke to me several times and used the library's public computers, printers, and maps, etc. to aid in their search. I continued to see and speak with them in the library the following summer.

Their son's remains were located over a year after his disappearance in the forests surrounding our community. I attended a memorial for their son in the woods near to where he was found. The parents stopped by the library to say hello the following summer for one last visit to the area and to say thanks. They also revealed they were a couple again.

Thea Schoettgen
Bear Valley, CA

DISSERTATION BEYOND DEATH

This is a story about reference librarians, teaching faculty, and the academic community. It took place a dozen years ago, when digital reference materials were far less robust than they are now.

I was a subject specialist in the field of education when a faculty member came to me with a challenging assignment. He had been working with a terminally ill student so that she could complete her dissertation before she died. Unfortunately, despite their best efforts, she died just a few weeks short of graduation. Her advisor wanted to complete the final, minor changes to the dissertation so that it could be submitted by the end of the semester, as University rules only allowed for posthumous award of a degree in the semester of the student's death. If the dissertation could be submitted within the next 72 hours, her family would be able to receive her degree in her memory; if it couldn't, they would not.

The issue was this: While her advisor had recovered most of her final drafts from her computer, her reference list was missing. And so, the question was: Can you successfully reconstruct an entire dissertation's worth of references using only the APA-style, in-text citations as your guide, and can you do it in 72 hours?

The answer was, with my knowledge of the field

and my access to a wealth of print and online reference tools, yes, I could (I missed 3, and her advisor made the minor changes necessary to remove the need for those citations). I spent the whole 72 hours I had to do the work (although that's not the sort of "reference question" our standard data collection tools are equipped to handle), the dissertation was submitted, and the student's family got her degree a week later. I was really impressed by her advisor and his commitment to helping his students finish their degrees; a few years later, he became my advisor.

And so, as I tell my students, don't ever think that reference services don't make a difference to people; they make a difference every day.

Scott Walter
Chicago, IL

HELPING STUDENTS

Assisting students is such a regular staple of library service that it seems hardly worthy of mention. Unfortunately, that mode of thinking makes it easy to neglect the very real impact librarians have on student success. The three stories here demonstrate understanding, acceptance, and trustworthiness in responding to student needs. Interestingly, school librarians bring these qualities, as well as a teaching credential, to their jobs, and yet many across the country are consistently (and tragically, for the students) at risk of getting cut. After you read this chapter, I urge you to check in on the status of your local school librarians and, if the need is there, mobilize in their defense. Every school should have a librarian!

A FLOOD OF MOTIVATION

Jennifer (not her real name) came to us almost a year into her Associate Degree program. Frankly, my coworkers and I had no idea how she had made it this far.

She had little grasp of proper grammar and spelling, and she openly plagiarized whole swathes of text from erroneous Google searches that led her to answers that didn't ever quite fit the questions asked.

She had to try to concentrate while babysitting her four grandsons: who were shooting their way through zombie hordes on the library's xBox and begging for dollars for the vending machine.

Especially on slow nights, I couldn't justify restricting her to the one-hour maximum slotted for 'book-a-librarian' appointments. But I exhausted myself trying to correctly identify when she actually needed my help versus when she was just burned out and wanting me to do the work for her.

After months, Jennifer was making slow but steady improvements, and almost finished with the Gen Ed requirements. And then one of our ceiling pipes burst... flooding the department and forcing us to close the building for over a week.

On re-opening day, Jennifer was already in a study room by the time I arrived for my shift; she had, of course, pre-booked an appointment with me.

But rather than a frantic call for help, I was met with a wide smile and an invitation to sit down while she told me about how, during my absence, she had stayed focused by "...imagining [me] as an angel on her shoulder."

Jennifer still needs my help on a regular basis, but now she comes to me with her assignments near completion only asking me for some of "my energy" to help her push through the last steps. Now that makes the flood (almost) worth it!

Ann Santori

WHAT MRS. JOHNSON TAUGHT

I was born with a mild physical disability. While in Middle School, I was excused from PE and sent to the library for study hall. Mrs. Johnson, the librarian took me under her wing. She taught me to "Question" what now is "Everything". But the most important lesson was *how* to *answer* those *questions*. Times have changed, but I know how and where to look.

I'm 62 now, and will never forget her. ♥

Kitty Brown
Dayton, OR

BUYING A PAPER

A tired middle-aged woman came up to the reference desk at the community college library where I work. She was hesitant and said:

"I don't even know if I should be asking this because I'm not sure about it..." but I told her all questions were welcome. She finally blurted out, "How would you go about buying a paper?"

I was stunned silent for a moment, but I recovered and managed to say:

"Why do you ask?" She said her professor made a comment in class about how if you buy your paper, make sure it contains quality research. Hearing her story, I presume he was making a joke, but she didn't know what to think of his comment. I fumbled for words as I looked at her nervous face and tried to figure out what kind of answer I could give. Finally I gave her a smile and said that while there are ways to buy papers, there are some big problems with that. We had a conversation about plagiarism, paper mills, and college rules, and she was near tears at the end. She said she hasn't been in school for over a decade and was feeling overwhelmed and out of her element. She genuinely thought (and hoped, I suspect) maybe there was some new method for papers. She gave an embarrassed laugh, and I made a joke about things sounding too good to be true, just to show her it was okay.

I talked a little about how we can help at the library when she has to do a paper and what other resources are on campus for her. She left looking a little less stressed.

Jennifer Lau-Bond
Evanston, Illinois, USA

ESSAY

LIBRARIES ARE NOT FREE, AND THEY'RE WORTH EVERY DOLLAR

It's tiresome. Every time a public library asks voters for a small tax increase, the anti-tax fundamentalists start hollering. I call them fundamentalists because their opposition to taxes is beyond rational; these are people who oppose any tax, no matter what:

- Roads full of potholes? No! no! no!
- Schools dealing with a huge increase in new residents? No! no! no!
- Firehouse could use some upgrades? No! no! no!
- 70-year-old library building needs to be replaced? No! no! no!

They're the people who will tell you, with a straight face, that they shouldn't have to cover those things because they don't drive on those roads, haven't any children in school, have never called the fire department, and don't use the library. In fact, they'll look right back at you and declare that taxes should be lowered for them. It's astounding!

One has to wonder, when the collection basket comes around at church, do they take money out? I mean, well, they gave 10% of their income two weeks ago, but they missed church last Sunday, so aren't they entitled to a refund? Plus, the church is raising money to replace the pews and, well, they don't use all of pews, so why should they pay for their replacement? It's a legitimate question for anti-taxxers: Should they support the common good of the congregation or buy a new jacuzzi for the master bedroom?

But maybe I'm going too far. Household budgets are stretched pretty thin for a lot of people. I can understand that; when I was growing up, the majority of our toys came from Goodwill. My parents worked 12-hour days to keep our family in the basics—we weren't impoverished, but I look back with amazement at what personal sacrifices they made to make ends meet. That said, no matter how little we had, my father dutifully wrote checks when the school booster club asked for funds. And he never complained about paying taxes.

Did my parents like taxes? Probably not. But they understood the fundamental idea that it was due to taxes that our weekly trips to the library, school lunches for me and my brother, medical care for my mother's aging parents, and a myriad other services, were possible. It's that simple. So when, in my teens, I began working and I noticed a certain amount of my meager paychecks being put aside for taxes, I didn't complain either.

Do I like taxes? Not particularly. But as my parents, and a great deal of other people in the United States, understand: Our country, individual states, and cities work, in part, because we do our part to support the common good. Taxes are an investment in the whole society, not just the rich or the poor, black or white, native-born or immigrant, old or young.

And libraries are the perfect example of how taxes are a smart investment. You see, those weekly library trips of my youth were only possible thanks to the generosity of the taxpayers in the City of Los Angeles!

Yes, it's true. Libraries are not free. And yet, unlike so many other ways to spend, it's pretty much impossible to argue against them from a financial perspective.

I don't know exactly what percentage of our parent's tax payments supported the local library, but I am certain that it cannot possibly compare to the cost of the piles of books my brother and I went through every week. Nor is it equivalent to the enriching library programs we attended, lessons in responsibility we learned from having our own library cards (see: https://tinyurl.com/ ResponsibleKids), or the ultimate pay-off: That thanks to the library, we became lifelong learners. Talk about long-term investment.

The average household in the United States pays $7.50 per month for their library. Is that a lot? It's hard to tell. So let's consider it in comparison with services comparable to what the library offers:

- Books: A James Patterson hardcover, *The People vs. Alex Cross* (release date: November 20th, 2017), was on sale at Amazon for $18.90. That's more than two months of library service. You may have to wait for the newest Patterson to come to the library, but you have access to thousands of other thrillers in the meantime. And with so many libraries offering ebooks, you don't even have to leave the house to take advantage of what your taxes cover.

- Music: A single CD, say Taylor Swift's *Reputation*, is $12.97 on Amazon. That's more than a month of a library where you get tons of CDs at your beck and call. Most people, though, subscribe to streaming music services like Spotify (Premium: $9.99), Tidal (basic Premium: $9.99), or others for their music. That's fine, many libraries offer streaming music through services like Freegal or Hoopla, complete with smartphone apps. Personally, I love Hoopla and use it all the time.

- Audiobooks: Individual audiobooks on CD are very expensive (think $50–$60 per book) and a basic Audible subscription is $14.95 a month. Libraries have both physical audiobooks and streaming services like Overdrive/Libby, Hoopla, RBDigital, and more! For your information, you don't have to pay extra for any of those—they're simply available to you as a taxpayer.

- Movies: A single feature film DVD is anywhere from $10–20, a basic subscription to Netflix is $7.99/month, Hulu is $7.99/month, and don't even get me started on the monthly cost of cable or satellite for your TV. Libraries have DVDs, streaming services like Hoopla, Kanopy, Digitalia, and more. Plus, most have monthly feature-film screenings with discussion.

- Internet Access: Like with cable/satellite service for TV, this is a sore spot for a lot of people. Most people pay anywhere from $20–$140 per month for internet access. Pretty much every library gives you internet access with a library card. Some don't even require that.

Most households pay for one (or more) of these services every single month. Individually, they cost more than the average month of library service, but if you start adding everything up, it quickly becomes obvious that the price of library service is insignificant compared to what most households spend on similar services. This is not even taking into account that libraries increase surrounding property values, are good for economic activity, and serve as a source of pride for communities. They are outstanding for educational attainment, often serve as an archive for local heritage, and are open to all. Multiple studies demonstrate that for every one dollar invested in libraries, there is a return-on-investment (ROI) of four or five dollars (see: https://tinyurl.com/LibraryROIStudies).

Taking into account everything you get from a tax-supported public library, it is completely obvious to everyone (except maybe the anti-taxxers) that libraries are a smart investment.

HUMOR

What's so funny about libraries? Well, it's not so much about libraries as an institution, but that we serve humans, and humans, when left to their own devices, tend to be hilarious. In this chapter are four amusing selections that showcase this. And if you're interested in more library humor, search out the work of librarian and humorist Roz Warren. She brings the goods.

BUILDING 666

After the devastating Northridge, California earthquake in January, 1994, our campus at California State University, Northridge, which was a mile from the epicenter of the quake, was virtually destroyed. It took six years before our beautiful Oviatt Library was completely re-opened.

In the early days following the quake, library faculty and staff worked in many locations all over campus, primarily in bungalows. My first assignment following the quake was in a bungalow answering the many phone calls that were coming in and trying to assure students that the spring semester would not be canceled.

Indeed, thanks to the leadership of CSUN President, Blenda Wilson, and the perseverance and determination of administration, faculty, staff, and students, classes started only two weeks late in bungalows all over campus and 6,700 students graduated in the first week of June (at the Hollywood Bowl, no less).

Each bungalow had an address sign and ours was "Building 666." Whoever was responsible for that we will never know, but our sign soon became a much pilfered item! During the time that we worked there, it was stolen several times. (See the Bible's Book of Revelation for clarification on "666!")

One day a student walked into our bungalow and

asked with a straight face, "Is this the Satanic Studies Department?"

Before all of us could burst out laughing, one of our very quick-witted staff shot back, "No! This is information from Hell!"

That kind of humor and camaraderie got us through the next six years until the grand re-opening of our much-missed Oviatt Library in July, 2000.

Margie Roblin
Northridge, CA

OOMPA LOOMPA CONNECTION

I spend 9 hours a week on duty in the "Quiet Room" of the community college library where I work. It is my job to maintain absolute silence in the room. This fall, a new student began coming in every day and he was having trouble with the "absolute silence" concept. He'd come in with a variety of friends several times a week, but he was always the common denominator. They'd be laughing, their cell phones would ring, or music would be blaring from their ear buds. Over and over I asked him to be quiet, and the tension escalated day after day. I finally said, in additional to pointing out the collaborative study areas as I usually did, that I needed him to start respecting the purpose of the room, his fellow students who were trying to learn and to study, and me. He did not take it well.

On the day before Halloween, a colleague and I dressed up as Willie Wonka and an Oompa-Loompa (me) and went around campus busting into classrooms where I would break into my original Ooompa Loompa song: "What do you get when you procrastinate? Subpar work and a paper that's late." As I was performing in one room I spotted this new student. He was smirking, trying hard not to laugh and shaking his head, as if to confirm my ridiculousness. Busted, I thought, disrespecting someone else's room.

Early Monday morning, he came into the quiet room, looked at me, smirked and shook his head. Then he proceeded to sit down at a table, alone, and study quietly. I had connected with him and that made the orange greasepaint worthwhile.

Donna Chandler
Fresno, CA

SHOWING OFF

When the ink on my MLS degree was still wet, back in the 1970s, I found a job at the public library in Wayne, New Jersey. I was a government documents librarian, but one afternoon a week it was my job to run the Children's Room.

That's where I was one day when two women walked in. At a glance I guessed that they were mother and grown daughter. It was the mother who was marching toward me with a determined look that said I'm going to get an answer if I have to stay here until you close the building around me. Librarians love that look.

She stopped in front of my desk and announced: "There's this book."

"Okay," I said.

"It's about... a tree."

And clearly, that was all she had. No author. No title. Just a memory of the book and a vital need to find it.

I admit I milked the moment. Can you blame me?

I stood up. "Follow me."

We paraded to the Easy Readers section and I bent down to the S's, and brought up The Giving Tree by Shel Silverstein.

The mother's jaw dropped. "That's it! How did you know?"

I shrugged. "I'm a librarian."

Mother and daughter walked off, arm in arm, to read a book and probably have a talk about what it meant to be a parent. I sat down at the desk and thought maybe I had picked the right profession.

Robert Lopresti
Western Washington University Libraries (retired)

THE GREATEST HITS OF BAD REFERENCE QUESTIONS

The phrase "there is no such thing as a bad question" is meant to both put the information-seeker at ease while, at the same time, sparking discussion on a given topic. There are, however, occasions where even the most experienced of librarians are taken aback by a library patron who manages to hit another level of bizarre in both content and detail of the question.

This level of bizarre occurred two years ago while I was volunteering at two large urban public libraries where I encountered a patron seeking some very specific information about the funeral arrangements for actress Annette Funicello. As I assisted this patron with locating the reference desk, I was awestruck by the detailed information being requested (e.g. location, time), as though he were a close friend or family member.

Later, after he thanked me for my help and walked out of the library satisfied with his printouts, I remember thinking about my newfound appreciation for the reference librarians who manage to maintain their composure and sense of professionalism while what they would really like to do is point out the oddities in both the question being asked and the amount of detail requested.

I also appreciated that the librarians with whom I spoke during that week were each willing to share their own versions of "The Greatest Hits of Bad Reference Questions." Up until that point, I had the impression that it was all-business among reference librarians, which made that rare behind-the-scenes moment of sharing all the more memorable.

Jeannine Berroteran
South Saint Paul, MN

JOB ASSISTANCE

Libraries get a lot of press for helping people with all aspects of the job search during difficult economic times, and it's true, libraries tend to be the busiest during downturns (not only helping people find jobs, by the way). Yet, it's also true that libraries help people find work no matter the state of the economy. These three stories show a few perspectives on what that assistance looks like.

BACK TO WORK

Having worked in libraries in big cities and small towns over the years, I am always amazed at the way that library staff can impact people and their lives. One evening as I was working at the reference desk, an older gentleman approached me looking for an electrical exam test prep book for a job test he was taking the next day.

As I was searching for the book, he shared with me that he had been out of the workforce for 20 years and his wife had recently passed away from cancer. He expressed to me that he was worried about whether his jobs skills would still be useful and his concerns about becoming employed again after such a long time. Although I was unable to find him a book in the library, I was able to recommend some websites which had the information he was seeking. He thanked me and left.

The next week, while I was doing community outreach at our local farmers market, he approached the library's booth with a huge smile. As he shook my hand, he shared with my co-workers that thanks to my assistance, he passed his test and was offered a job that same day. Through helping this man and countless others, I feel so grateful for the opportunity to help people, provide assistance and act as a positive change agent in their lives.

Tamara Evans
Hanford, CA

MONDAY MORNINGS

For over a decade, I was the Director at a very rural library located in the northeastern corner of Vermont. During that time, the large furniture factory that had employed a big part of the area for years closed. With the large amount of unemployed persons in such a remote area, a special unemployment office was established in a nearby town and served the displaced workers for some time. When the temporary office packed up and left, many still-unemployed residents were left to file weekly unemployment claims by either driving over an hour away every week or filing via the Internet. The problem was that a good percentage of these unemployed folks did not have the Internet at home or any computer skills.

Consequently, the library began to fill every Monday upon opening with folks needing one-on-one help. With only myself and one part-time staff person, this became extremely stressful for all involved. With the library trustee's support and a few extra hours allotted for my assistant, we began to open an hour earlier on Monday mornings for unemployment filers only. This allowed us to privately help each filer needing assistance.

The gratitude we received from these weekly patrons was more than worth the extra effort.

Deborah Gadwah
Canaan, VT

NEW LUNCH LADY

I work as a Youth Services Librarian at a public library, but this story involves my assisting another adult who works with children.

A customer came to me for assistance with a job application. This customer had moved to the United States from Cuba. She spoke very little English, and did not have much computer knowledge. She was applying for a job as a Substitute Cafeteria Employee – she would be working at various school cafeterias covering for absent employees upon request.

I assisted her both in filling out the application as well as with translating from Spanish to English. Most of the assistance was conducted in Spanish.

A few weeks later, she came to thank me for my help. Why? She obtained the job!

A few months after that, she came into the library again to share even better news. She had obtained a full-time position in a school's cafeteria! It was an important break for her; the higher salary, benefits, and stability that came with this new job really benefited both the customer and her daughter. But she didn't stop there, thanks to the library, the new lunch lady began learning English and bettering her computer skills.

Heidi Colom
Tampa, FL

ESSAY

WHY THE VALUE OF SELF-RELIANCE IS AT THE HEART OF LIBRARIES

I recently re-read Ralph Waldo Emerson's timeless essay "Self-Reliance" and found it different then what I remembered. Emerson's self-reliance is rigidly individualistic, non-conformist, and solitary; a person must invent their own ideas, everyone else be damned. This differs slightly from our colloquial ideas of self-reliance as either self-made in a materialistic sense or the quality of a person who has achieved a lot through hard work ("...blood, sweat, and tears."). When we think of a self-reliant individual, many of us picture a pioneer-type in the Wild West, venturing out to explore the untamed wilderness and surviving to tell the tale. While not untrue in its essence, one may simply point out that though this person existed in the past, the West has been won. To that end, it must be asked: What is self-reliance in contemporary life?

I would say that today's vision of self-reliance looks

like a single mother working three jobs to support her family, a student staying up nights studying to be the first in their family to graduate with a university degree, or a small business owner stretching themselves thin to keep a company going. The self-reliance these everyday heroes demonstrate is in their iron resolve – an internal flame that keeps them working hard despite the odds. Does self-reliance mean that outside forces can't make their endeavors easier? I don't think so. Indeed, the library can aid all three without tarnishing their self-reliant credibility.

Our self-reliant single mother could, for example, bring her kids to the library when she has a moment. There, they will have access to high-quality reading material and educational programming (that's also fun). And if the kids are old enough to go to the library on their own after school, chances are they will be able to spend time with peers and do their homework until until their mother finishes work for the evening.

If she can find the energy and motivation between child-rearing and work, there are library resources readily available to help her develop useful job skills. She could start with books and audiobooks related to general office work or whatever field she's in, but she needn't stop there. Many libraries now offer free access to top-notch online training courses including, but not limited to, Gale Courses and Lynda.com for those who want to improve on their own schedule.

Our starving student is no less lucky to have the

library at his side while he sits and studies. Most students seek a solitary study spot away from the potential distractions of home or friends. Many soak in knowledge at their university libraries, but public libraries serve this purpose as well. Most have special study rooms available to reserve, free internet access, login info for research databases, and erudite librarians ready to assist. Does asking for a librarian's aid hinder self-reliance? Not at all! A student can ask a single question and be shown skills that will make their future information-seeking quicker and more efficient.

Of course, there's nothing that says a bona-fide lone wolf can't also use the library on their own. In the modern library, most gates are open—people are welcome to come in, look around, get what they need. Yet, a time-pressed student is best to weigh the potential time spent on an initial independent search, with the time that can be saved by asking a librarian now and gaining a well-deserved independence in the future.

And the small business owner? I didn't forget her. Over there creating marketing materials, making sales calls, keeping the books, and (if there's time) thinking about strategic planning, to name a few tasks she does in a single afternoon. Can the library help this self-starting entrepreneur win the business game? For sure!

I've written in the past how small business owners can freely access market research data at the library (see: https://tinyurl.com/LibraryMarketResearch), and others have highlighted many a winning partnership between the library and business communities (see: "Libraries and the Business Community: A Success Story," (https:// tinyurl.com/LibrariesAndBusiness) "A Day in the Life of a Small Business Specialist,"(https://tinyurl.com/ SmallBizSpecialist) and "As a Business Librarian, I Help People Find Their Passion,"(https://tinyurl.com/ BusinessLibrarian) for a few examples) so I won't rehash all that.

Instead I'm going to take you back to the beginning of my library career. At the time, my life was hectic: I was in graduate school full-time, working 20-hours a week shelving books at one library, freelancing as an archivist and web projects coordinator at a radio archive, and running a small side business as a computer consultant. Oh, and I was also interning at another library. It was at this internship where I had the chance to run a 30-minute brown-bag lunchtime seminar on "Blogging for Business."

It wasn't a big deal, I prepared a presentation on the basics of blogging platforms, how to develop an audience, and ways a blog could help a business. We went well over the designated thirty minutes in what turned out to be a incisive and personal discussion. The audience (a few local business owners) and I were able to mull over options that were individual to them. I enjoyed sharing my experience, and they got a free, no-string-attached, consultation.

This is what a library offers to small business owners, beyond the plethora of resources in book stacks and on servers. Whereas everyone else wants a piece, the library exists to add a piece. Often with a smile and the personal touch.

Does the self-reliant individual shy away from such a place? Never that. True self-reliants use whatever resources they can to become even more self-reliant. It's no wonder so many of history's greatest auto-didacts made libraries their second home.

Emerson wrote, "What I must do is all that concerns me, not what the people think. This rule, equally arduous in actual and in intellectual life, may serve for the whole distinction between greatness and meanness. It is the harder because you will always find those who think they know what is your duty better than you know it. It is easy in the world to live after the world's opinion; it is easy in solitude to live after our own; but the great man is he who in the midst of the crowd keeps with perfect sweetness the independence of solitude."

With that in mind, count on the fact that no ludicrous remarks diminishing libraries will affect my goodwill towards them. But don't take my word for it, stick to the Emersonian approach to self-reliance and discover a love of libraries for yourself!

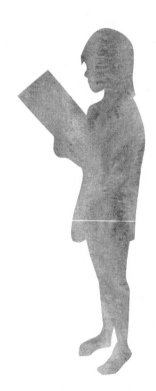

KINDNESS

The epitome of what makes library work worthwhile are the opportunities to help people when they are most in need. Every library worker has a choice in this regard: In the face of someone struggling, stick to your job as written, or be a refuge to someone. I am thankful that so many library workers choose the latter approach. While all of the stories in this book contain kindness, the ones in this chapter have it as the central premise. Ready your tissues!

A WINTER HAT AND GLOVES

Today, I had a young woman come into my library looking quite disheveled, distressed, and very cold and wet. It had been snowing here all day.

While getting her a guest card to use a computer, I commented on how she needed a winter hat, and she informed me that she'd just been released from jail and needed to get home to the city (which was over 100 miles away).

After she'd been on the computer for a few minutes I noticed that she'd begun to cry. It seemed that she was having a very hard time getting anyone to come pick her up, especially with the bad weather and potentially icy roads.

I tried to offer her a hot coffee to warm her up, but she said she was fine, still sniffling. A little while later, I had the chance to leave the building and ran to the local thrift store. I picked her up a winter hat and a pair of warm gloves. When I returned and handed the bag to her she cried again, but this time with gratitude.

We let her stay at the computer longer by giving her a second guest card when the time on her first ran out, and eventually she was able to get an aunt to come and pick her up. We sent her on her way with a certificate for a free hamburger and dessert at the local McDonalds, which she accepted graciously.

Before she left, she asked us if we accepted donations. She had good books that she wanted to bring us the next time she was in the area.

Anonymous

FIRST TOY

While providing youth services at the Pittsburgh, CA branch of the Contra Costa County Library system as a long-term substitute, I was asked to run a series of craft programs as part of the Summer Reading Program. It was around the Fourth of July, when I was leading one of these programs at which kids made fun take-home projects. That day, the children were creating two projects: I don't remember the first, but the second was a handmade tambourine with small jingle bells.

It was a popular event and many excited children rushed into the children's area to make the projects, all except three quiet and sad-looking kids, who walked in slowly. After all the coloring was finished, the bells attached, streamers glued in place, the large group of participants began to leave. All except for those three sad children who came together. They sat at a table coloring a picture. When finished, they came to me, clutching their tambourines, and the youngest boy said, "Thank you. This will be my first toy since the fire."

I knelt down to hear the full story and look at the picture they had drawn me. Apparently, fireworks had caused a house fire and they had lost everything, including their pets. I will never forget their happiness hugging those handmade "toys" to their chests. I thanked them for sharing their picture and story with me and wished in my heart that I could give them more. They left smiling and laughing, which is all I could have hoped for.

Alyson Matthews

FRIDAY FLICKS

We have a monthly film series called "Friday Flicks" at my public library where we show a newly released film to adults on a Friday afternoon. One of our regular attendees is an older woman who has some difficulty hearing and reminds me each time about turning on the closed captioning (I always do anyway, just in case there is anyone in the audience who needs it but is too embarrassed to ask).

On one particular month, while I was getting the refreshments ready before beginning the movie, the woman came to the back of the room and was chatting with me. She was really looking forward to the movie because she'd heard how good it was from others. She told me how glad she was that I always turned on the closed captions because at other places, they would get upset if she asked. I told her how horrible that was and that I, as a 37-year-old with normal hearing, even found captions useful sometimes if I couldn't understand what was said during a film.

It was then that she revealed to me that the reason she enjoyed coming to "Friday Flicks" so much was because she couldn't see any of the new movies in theaters, because theaters didn't offer closed captioning. I told her that most theaters had devices available for people who are hard of hearing, but she said those devices didn't help her.

Up to that point, I hadn't fully considered just how important a simple film program could be to some people. This interaction really drove that point home.

Michelle M.
Franklin Park, IL

SAFE SHELTER

Saturday mornings are generally very busy at the library. However, this Saturday was unusually quiet. That is, until a young woman wearing a thick winter coat and beanie approached me at the desk. She asked if she could get a library card and, handing her the form, I asked a routine question: Is the address on your I.D. current? Her answer was no.

This woman in the warm wool jacket explained that she had been living in her car for the past two weeks since her father passed away. She didn't feel safe at the local homeless shelter because some of the men made crude remarks towards her. She said she really only wanted a library card for computer access so that she could write a resume and apply for jobs.

Once I finished creating her new account, I also handed her a small plastic card with the names and locations of resources for those struggling with homelessness. Her eyes lit up when she noticed a women's shelter was listed. As she took her new library card and before she headed off to the computers, the young woman expressed her gratitude for the library—a place to write a resume, a place to find safe shelter, a place that could offer her hope that things can get better.

Amellia Fiske
Napa Valley, CA

HE REMEMBERS ME?

I am a Library Assistant at Oakland Public Library (OPL) and met Daryl when I was facilitating writing workshops in the county juvenile hall with The Beat Within and the Oakland Youth Poet Laureate program.

Daryl is currently incarcerated in the juvenile hall and will probably be transferred to a state juvenile facility in a few months when he turns 18. I found out Daryl used to go to OPL's Brookfield branch library and knew Alfred, the Library Assistant there. I encouraged Daryl to write to Alfred.

Alfred has been Brookfield's Library Assistant since 4-year-old Daryl first started coming to the library. Alfred remembers him as a smart, respectful, well-behaved, and mature boy who would make sure his sisters treated the library and the books with respect.

Alfred was really glad to hear from Daryl, though sorry about his current circumstances. Daryl was very touched to receive a reply from Alfred and to know that he was remembered. Alfred suggested that Daryl ask his family to bring his daughters by the library so Alfred could meet them. Daryl promised he would. Alfred now keeps Daryl in mind and thinks about which projects and activities he can send to him.

This exchange would not have happened without a library worker making a regular effort to link individual incarcerated youth with the public library. The interaction showed Daryl that he makes a good and lasting impression on people and is cared about even if he's made mistakes with significant consequences. Hopefully this experience will also give his daughters a connection to the library and a wider community.

Peggy Simmons
Oakland Public Library (CA)

PAYING IT FORWARD

Something that is not often covered in library ROI studies is the library's long-term impact on empowering community members to use the skills, knowledge, and/or motivation they picked up at the library to further serve the community. In this chapter, this is exhibited via a teen volunteer, a literacy student-turned-tutor, and a mother passing on a love of libraries to her kids.

ANNIE SPEAKS

Annie was a teen volunteer at the library. She started as a shelver and then moved to our Homework Center. In January 2015, she joined a pilot group tasked with creating S.T.E.A.M. Maker Boxes for teen programs. She informed me she'd like to participate in all aspects of the pilot but would not speak in front of a group. Though I accepted her restriction, throughout the six-month pilot, I offered her opportunities that allowed her to move toward public speaking.

First, she agreed to write the text for other people to deliver. Next, she agreed to stand next to presenters and add a comment if the presenter forgot something. After that, she sat beside a facilitator at an in-house Mini Maker Faire and help explain procedures for the event. At the end of the six months, Annie was comfortably co-facilitating programs!

While the pilot ended, Annie continued to participate in our Maker events, and was soon able to facilitate a table without aid. But let Annie's July 2015 words speak for themselves regarding the importance of our program to her:

"This program has inspired me in various different ways:

One, for once in my life, I saw a hint, a mere spark of interest, that perhaps public speaking could actually be fun! I am a little more comfortable speaking in front of people than I was when I first started out. That is not to say that I don't still have a long ways to go, but at least it feels a little more doable than before.

Two, the program has reignited a curious spark in me; I want to know "why" and "how" for everything. Unlike school has conditioned me to think, believe it or not, learning can be a bucket of fun.

Lastly, this program has taught me a more broad lesson: Take chances, go out and say "yes" more! This thought will have a tremendous influence in my personal growth and development."

In the summer of 2017, Annie went to Taiwan and was "...placed to teach junior high kids (7th and 8th grade). This program is a government-funded program that trains volunteers for one week, then we go out and teach at our various assigned schools for two weeks with lesson plans we design ourselves..."

Annie is paying it forward.

Gail Stovall
West Sacramento, CA

LEARNING OUT LOUD

"When I first came to Literacy Connects [a literacy program that often uses public libraries as its base], I was afraid and embarrassed. Then things started changing. I changed too. Now I am confident and proud to be learning. Every place is a good place to learn. It doesn't matter where you are or how short the chairs are."

Librarian Rebecca Howey (now retired) adds: Beginning in 2010, Uwe and I met every week at the library. One Sunday in 2011, the only available seats were in the children's area, but Uwe decided that learning was more important to him than staying embarrassed. We sat in the giraffe chairs and worked. No one stared, and anyone who cared thought, "That's cool!" Uwe wanted to re-enact our adventure to show other students they don't need to be afraid to learn out loud; a student assistant at the library took photos.

Uwe's words from the beginning of this entry appeared in the student literary magazine and other Literacy Connects publications. Since then, Uwe has written more essays, stories, and poems, read more books and poems, learned to multiply and divide, flown cross country (through Dallas-Fort Worth) without help, reprogrammed his cable remote, read the instructions and replaced a part on his pool pump, been honored at work for his accomplishments and attitude, learned to play the guitar, started a book club for adult learners, spoken to state legislators and large audiences about the importance of adult education opportunities, acted on stage, been the subject of features on television and radio, volunteered yearly at the Tucson Festival of Books, met his favorite author, Mitch Albom, and become a tutor himself, helping adult learners of English. Last week he emailed the mayor about roads in Tucson and got a reply. Uwe's motto is: Go as far as you can, and then just keep going.

Uwe Keilitz
Tuscon, AZ

Uwe Keilitz and former Literacy Connects staff, Leslie Pape

THE LIBRARY: A WHOLE NEW WORLD

Growing up in the ghetto of south central Los Angeles, I was surrounded by crime, violence and people with no aspirations, dreams or future. It was not safe to be outside and traveling to and from school was a terrifying time. Besides TV, I had no other entertainment, but I always had a love for words and stories, and learning new things. Thanks to school, I was introduced to my first library.

I also had a friend who would bring me books from home to occupy my time after school. I always completed my homework in record time and had many hours left to do nothing but fear going outside or listen to the dismaying conversations of the adults in the home. Thanks to the books my friend loaned me, I had a distraction. I would read and finish the books, and return them the very next day. I read so fast that she had to start bringing me two or more books at a time.

Once I had access to the school library, I spent a lot of time there during the school day, often skipping recess and lunch just to be in there with the books. During my high school years at Manual Arts, I was in the library book club and spent a lot of time discovering new books and information about the world as I prepared for adulthood.

When I left for college, I also went to my first public

library, the Arcata Library in Northern California. It never dawned on me that I had not been to a public library in all of 18 years living in Los Angeles! The excitement of being able to check out books as many times as I wanted to was the most awesome thing ever.

Libraries have opened up a whole new world for me. Libraries gave me a home, a safe haven, a doorway into other worlds, cultures, and languages. If I had not had access to the library, I may not have known that there was a chance for me outside of the environment I grew up in. My children were brought up to share my love of books and a trip to the library was as necessary as going to school.

Every city that I've ever lived in, I sought out the library before any other local resource! That's how much libraries mean to me.

Shonquinta Jones
Arcata, CA

ESSAY

DAY IN THE LIFE: REFERENCE LIBRARIAN AT A PUBLIC LIBRARY

There are many different types of librarians. For years I served as an reference librarian serving adults, and occasionally kids, at a several libraries. Because a common question asked of librarians is "What do you actually do at your job?" I wanted to give you a typical day in the life of a reference librarian at a busy public library. Off we go!

9:00am—My day begins when I arrive at the library. Greeting my colleagues, I unpack my work bag, turn on the computer, and login to email. I can only read a message or two because we have a stand-up meeting in 15 minutes.

9:15am—In a large and busy library, a quick all-hands stand-up meeting is extremely useful to keep everyone apprised of the day's happenings. When all of the librarians, shelvers, desk clerks, and library assistants are gathered, the library manager goes through the staff schedule, gives a run-down of daily events (for example:

Toddler storytime at 11am, book club at 2pm, coding workshop at 5pm), and informs us of relevant city news and initiatives coming down the pike from library administration. By 9:30am, the meeting is over and everyone scatters to get ready for the day.

9:35am—Back in my cubicle, I work on email—coordinating a future Wikipedia editing workshop, following-up about a difficult reference question, reading a few posts from a library list-serv. Glancing over at the desk schedule, I notice that I'm due on the reference desk for the first two hours, from 10am-12pm (we open at 10am). It's 9:53am, meaning it's time to hustle out there and get everything set up.

9:55am—At my library, we have three public service desks: At the entrance is the circulation desk, where materials are checked-out, returned, and patrons handle account issues. In the children's area is the youth services information desk, where young people and parents go to ask reference questions. And upstairs, in the adult section, is the reference desk. That's where I work. There are two computers because our workload is such that it requires two staff members during much of the day.

When I arrive, I make sure I have a pen and note cards, and get the computer ready to go.

10:00am—The floodgates open! A crowd of people stomp up the stairs towards the public computers and to reserve study rooms. My colleague and I at the reference desk are immediately swamped. We sign people up for their study rooms and help others login to the computers.

10:05am—The phone rings. An impatient patron wants to know if we have a title on the shelf. Their tone suggests that I should know the answer without even checking, which is difficult since my library branch has tens of thousands of volumes. I look it up in the online catalog, and we do have it. "Would you like to me to set it aside for you?" "Yes, yes. I need it immediately!" So I put them on hold and go search for the book on the shelf (I always do this while the person is on hold, since sometimes the book turns out to be missing, and I don't want them to make a wasted trip). The book is on the shelf. I pull it and head back to the desk only to find that the patron hung up without giving me their name. I put a post-it on the book and let my colleague know that someone may be coming for it.

The next hour and ten minutes are a standard reference shift; I help people with computer issues, search for library materials, and answer reference questions on a variety of topics. Probably, I help 15 or 20 people, most of them with simple questions. It gets busier in the afternoon.

11:15am—A volunteer arrives! Aside from being a reference librarian, I also serve as the volunteer coordinator for my library, which means I am responsible for recruiting, interviewing, training, and scheduling volunteers. This volunteer works 4 hours a week on two different days. I explain today's assignment: Use a handheld scanner to go through the adult fiction section and pull the books that have an incorrect status (lost, missing, not in catalog, etc.).

Every volunteer has different skills and preferences. This young man likes working independently, so I give him assignments that are both useful for the library and enjoyable for him. In a couple of hours, he will likely find a few misplaced books which is satisfying to him and important for collection maintenance.

12:00pm—My desk shift is over! I head back to my cubicle to get a few things done before I take my lunch break at 1pm. It takes me a few minutes to get my bearings after working with the public for two hours. As a palate cleanser, I log-in to the library's Twitter—no replies that require responses since last time I checked. Seeing a post in my feed that would be interesting to library patrons, I re-tweet it.

In the following 40 minutes, I fill out my timesheet, read and answer emails, call a new volunteer who has passed a background check to schedule an orientation, and submit a few future library programs to our website calendar. It would be nice if my day included more deeply focused time, but in reality, with 4–5 daily hours on the reference desk, managing volunteers, organizing library programs, collection development, and chatting with colleagues, I end up doing many more small tasks than deep work. It's hard to find long periods of uninterrupted time working in a library!

1:00pm—Lunch time! I didn't bring lunch from home today so I head out for a meatball sandwich at pizza place down the street. Having worked at this library for the last couple of years, I'm on first-name basis with many of the local restaurant workers and baristas. Sometimes I eat lunch where they work, and sometimes they visit me at the library!

2:00pm—Back on the desk for another two-hour shift. I notice that the caller from this morning has not picked up their book. Oh, well.

About 30 minutes in, a regular patron stops in to chat about what she's been reading and what she should read next. In the library world, we call this book recommendation service "readers' advisory" (or RA) and it's a whole sub-field of library science with many books written on the topic (Joyce Saricks' *Readers Advisory in the Public Library*, and *Genreflecting*, edited by Diana Tixier Herald and Wayne Wiegand, are still on my shelf to this day). A good RA librarian has both a vast knowledge of books and the sensitivity to interview a patron and quickly determine what will appeal to them. Readers' advisory is one of my favorite parts of being a reference librarian, so it is especially gratifying when patrons return many times to continue our literary conversations.

As I'm on the reference desk, I should say that another aspect of librarianship I enjoy is reference service. People come to the library to ask questions about everything! Being competent at reference is a combination of at least two qualities: 1) Performing a solid reference interview, meaning an interaction specifically designed to work with the patron to determine their need—sometimes it's easy, and sometimes not so much (for an example, see #1 in the article "Three Lessons I've Learned About People from Being a Librarian" (https://tinyurl.com/ ThreeLessonsILearned)), 2) Having a wide-ranging knowledge of the information landscape; librarians know that a Google search is just one avenue of search, and that there are a many, many more. Often enough, when I'm asked a reference question, I can bypass a search and go straight to the correct resource, saving time and energy for all involved. Explanations aside, it was a busy reference shift; with readers advisory, reference questions, computer assistance, and more, the two hours flew quickly by.

4:00pm—I need a break so I pop over to the local coffee shop for an espresso and a chat with the barista.

4:15pm—Back at work it's time to prepare for my weekly drop-in coding workshop. Though I am not an expert programmer, I do have enough experience with fundamental programming concepts and building websites, to help people get started on their journey. More importantly, I have a good grasp of the variety of learning resources out there. Lucky for me, I also have an intelligent and personable volunteer co-leading the workshop. We set up tables and chairs, loaner laptops, a few useful books, and are ready to go.

5:00pm—The workshop begins. Since it's an open-ended drop-in program, people come at different times and for different reasons. Today, we get a couple of newbies started on beginner lessons, I help a local blogger figure out the intricacies of customizing his WordPress site, and a few people come in to learn mostly on their own (asking the occasional questions). The average attendance of the workshop is 5–10, with some coming weekly, some every month, and some just once or twice. Aside from individual learning, the purpose of this program is to establish a community of practice—the fact that ours is a social learning space is part of what differentiates it from the numerous excellent tutorials available online.

6:15pm—The workshop is winding down, we begin to put away the loaner laptops and tidy the space. People are asking their final questions and finishing up.

6:25pm—I'm back in my cube chatting with my supervisor about the workshop went. He brings up an issue we had with a difficult patron earlier and we discuss how to handle that person in the future. The day is winding down, I give my email a final check, and pack up my stuff.

6:55pm —I go out onto the floor to help with the walk-through. Ours is a large library with many places to hide so we are diligent about sweeping the place. Anyway, spending the night would be pretty difficult with our building alarm wailing.

7:00pm —The library is closed. I go to the office and grab my stuff. We do a final sweep and head downstairs to set the alarm. That done, we say our goodbyes and head home. No two days are exactly alike at the library. Between the variety of duties librarians have and the fact of working with the public, being a reference librarian at a public library is an adventure!

AT THE REFERENCE DESK

Reference, Information, "Ask Us", and countless other names are used in the library world to refer to that place where librarians sit answering the public's questions. It's also where the potential for magic is at its strongest. The perceptive, encouraging, and intelligent contributors of the stories in this section show how life-changing a simply query can be when handled by a caring librarian.

A SAFE PERSON TO TALK TO

I was the teen librarian at a busy public library. Because I know how important it is for GLBTQ teens to have safe adults to talk to, I put a rainbow sticker on my nametag and hung a similar symbol from the flash drive I always had plugged into the computer monitor when I worked the reference desk. During my time there, no teen ever approached me with any sensitive issues, but an adult did.

One of our regular patrons came to the desk and began asking me personal questions. They had noticed that I wore the rainbow, but also a wedding ring, and had overheard me talking about my kids. They wanted to know, was I gay or not? I explained that I wore the rainbow as a symbol that I was a safe person to talk to, without answering the personal questions. They seemed satisfied.

About a week later the same patron approached the desk again and asked to speak with me privately. We adjourned to the empty computer lab, and there they told me their story. For most of their life they had been secretly cross-dressing. Though the patron presented publicly as male, she really felt that she was female. She wanted to know where she could learn more about being transgender and the process of transitioning.

I asked a few more questions, completing the

reference interview, and by the time she left she had a stack of books, a list of local organizations, and the biggest smile I had ever seen her wear.

Karl G. Siewert
Tulsa, OK

DO YOU HAVE A MINUTE?

I'd love to tell you about my friend Bill, an older gentleman who loves to learn but was having technology challenges. He would come in every afternoon with his laptop and we would go through our little ritual.

"Hi Courtney! Do you have a minute?"

"Sure, Bill! Come and get me when you're up and running."

We both knew it would be more than a minute. I'd go sit with him and help him download music, set up his Facebook account, enroll in online courses, order mock turtlenecks, and figure out the correct print margins as well as other tasks.

Bill didn't really need my computer expertise. What he really needed was someone who believed in him and could patiently walk him through the process; someone to assure him that he wasn't stupid; someone to boost his confidence.

Then one day it happened...Bill sheepishly told me he didn't need me anymore! He had a big grin on his face – the kind a child has the day the training wheels come off! Our new conversations start like this: "Hi Courtney! Guess what I was able to do all by myself?!"

Courtney Ann
Mount Shasta, CA

THE RIGHT BOOK

My first professional job as Mrs. Rabbitt, Children's Librarian, was at the public library in picturesque Peterborough, New Hampshire from 2001-2005.

One of my favorite customers, Peter, loved *Redwall* and was a member of my Redwall Club where we feasted each month on recipes from the series.

Peter's younger sister, Sylvia, was sweetly intent. She was eight years old when she got glasses for nearsightedness. Her mother asked for my help in finding a book or two that might help.

I recommended books, but none seemed quite perfect. I emailed a query into the remarkable land of a children's librarian list-serv. Elizabeth Bluemle, a "yet unpublished" author responded with a copy of her own manuscript about a little nearsighted girl named Iris. I passed it on to Silvia and her mother.

Fast forward to 2013 when Bluemle wrote a blog post in Shelf Talker in *Publisher's Weekly*. In it, she wrote that she had received an email from a now-grown up, seventeen-year old girl named Sylvia. Sylvia wrote of a time that her librarian gave her a "bunch of white paper clipped together." She added that her librarian told her that she was one of its first readers of a unique copy of a book. Sylvia felt cool. And she felt very special.

Sylvia went on to describe her librarian, Mrs. Rabbit (sic) who she said was "...one extraordinary world-class children's librarian." Long story short, another librarian found the Shelf-Talker blog post and sent it to me.

You won't be surprised that I sat and sobbed when I read it.

Sylvia's letter made my entire career as a librarian worth everything. I was merely doing the extraordinary – something children's librarians do every day. I put the right "book" in the right hands at the right time.

Charlotte Canelli
Norwood, MA

A TOUCH OF HISTORY

One day, when I worked at a small branch campus of a major academic library, I was trying to explain the difference between primary and secondary sources to a student.

He was researching slavery and I happened to know that we had a book about slavery from the 1800s in our rare book collection so I got the key and opened the case. I took the book to the young man and showed it to him as an example of a primary source. He looked at me and the book and asked:

"That book is from the 1800s?"

And I said, "Yes."

He asked if he could touch it and I gave it to him. He lightly fingered the pages and then looked at me and said "So when this was printed my ancestors were slaves?"

"Yes," I said.

There was a silence between us and I will never forget the look in his eyes or the moment of understanding between us. It gives me goosebumps to this day. I'm happy to say that he did well on his paper using both secondary and primary sources.

Rachel Stevenson

SPECIAL NEEDS

The title of this chapter is not about the physical or psychological disability or difference of the patrons in the stories. It is intended to highlight that in the library, everyone's needs are special and worthy of the time and effort it takes to be of service. These stories highlight what library workers do every day – make a difference in people's lives simply by being there and doing their jobs well.

"NOTHIN' BETTER'N A VETERAN!"

Mike served in the US Army during World War II. He was an old man in a wheelchair when I met him, but his military service still hugely defined his life—mostly because, as part of his service, he was blinded. But Mike never let his blindness stop his hunger for learning or for life.

Naturally, Mike was happy to discover the National Library Service for the Blind and Physically Handicapped. It's a free service of the Library of Congress, providing Braille and audio books by mail. From records to cassettes to the brand new digital audio player, which he was among the very first of our patrons to receive, and to the huge Braille book boxes arriving frequently at his home, Mike read, and read, and read. We at the Talking Book Library in Fresno kept him supplied with endless Louis L'Amour, WEB Griffin, Tom Clancy, and anything else a man's man like Mike loves to read.

Mike and his devoted wife and caregiver Susan were regular members of our Talking Book Library Book Club. He shared his wisdom and his life's learning with us, as well as sharing the doughnuts they brought every month, and the coffee, which he drank strong and black and with at least three Sweet 'N Lows. He relied on the library for his books, and we relied on him for his sweet and funny presence. We all loved Mike, and he loved the program and loved us.

Mike passed away a few years ago at over 90 years-old. It was my privilege to attend his military funeral and yes, there were a few tears shed. The library impacted Mike's whole life, and he impacted all of ours.

Wendy Eisenberg
Fresno, CA

A WIN WITH GAMING

I've been doing gaming tournaments at the library for a while now, and the response has generally been very good —there have been a lot of enthusiasm and big crowds.

While I was at the Perris (CA) Library, I was approached by the mother of one of the participants who thanked me for putting it on. She told me that her son was autistic, and that he never interacted with other children, but that at the tournament she saw him playing happily and talking with other kids.

The two of them became regulars at those programs, and she even provided snacks and drinks on her own dime for the participants. I'm glad we made a difference for them.

Thomas Vose
Oakland, MD

ANDREW

One of my regular groups at storytime was a daycare of five children. Four girls, and Andrew. Andrew would go where he was physically led, though would be silent and not participate. If we all stood up to sing, he sat silently. If we started to march, we marched around Andrew. If we moved to the tables to do a craft, his teacher would escort him to a chair and physically put the supplies in his hands, and he might do something like color or use a glue stick. Or not. It seemed to depend entirely on Andrew.

I could see Andrew looking at the pages of the books we read together. I could see that he was watching the puppets. When I asked if he wanted a sticker I might get a look that said "yes" and when I said "we need to put the crayons away now" he would put a few in the box with us.

One day, we were coloring after storytime. I was sitting between Andrew and one other child, working on our crafts. Andrew leaned over to me and whispered. "I can write my name" and then went back to coloring. I said, also in a whisper, "That's great Andrew, that you can write your name." That is the only conversation I ever had with Andrew.

Today, Andrew would get a diagnosis, and I would get instructions. As long ago as I was a children's librarian, there were no instructions, and Andrew was just Andrew. Welcome at the library, part of storytime, and proud to be able to write his name.

Hillary Theyer
Monterey, CA

LIBRARY MAGIC

One day, a three year-old boy and his mom came to Magician Dale Lorzo's performance at the library. Mom said it was the first time her boy had been in public with that many people (there were about 25). He was so shy, he would only sit in the far back. Dale entertained so well, though, and had such control of the room, that the boy responded to him like a bee to honey. The child and mom moved closer, right up to the front, and thoroughly enjoyed the show, although the boy pulled-in when the other children screamed.

They returned to the quiet of the library early. There, the boy relaxed and made a wand. Then, when the program ended and the loud kids arrived, he stuck with the crafts, even though his face was tense.

His mother told me that this was a big step towards handling people in public. She was appreciative, took a reading log, and said that they would be back for sure.

Susan Parsons
Arcata, CA

ESSAY

FIVE INTRIGUING REASONS WHY PUBLIC LIBRARY STAFF IS CRUCIAL TO COMMUNITIES

I recently read a study (see: https://tinyurl.com/ ProximityToBooks) in which researchers placed book-vending machines in "book deserts," or low-income neighborhoods where there was little access to books, and studied their use. What they found wasn't surprising: Access to books increased literacy and school-readiness. Even less surprising was this quote:

> "Our findings suggest that only having one side of the equation—access to books or adult support—is insufficient. Rather, both are necessary. Without access to books, one cannot read to children; without adult supports, children cannot be read to," said Neuman."

Reading this, my mind immediately went to libraries. There are misguided people that define libraries as

warehouses for books, and feel that this is enough.
What they fail to notice is an equally important
element of libraries— trained, specialized, engaging,
and enthusiastic library staff that connect young people
(and their parents) to age and skill-appropriate reading.
It is the people who labor there that make what would
otherwise be an simple item-storage place into a library.
Here are five intriguing reasons why:

1. Library staff know the community

Aside from the local historical society or university,
the public library is a place where you can come and
ask questions about a community's past and present. It's
not just because library workers often live in the area
they serve that this is the case. Indeed, I've worked in
many places where I did not live, but have always made
it a point to get to know the history and current events
of the town. Especially in close-knit communities, the
librarian (or clerk, or library assistant, or page) becomes a
weaver, connecting members of the area with each other
when the need arises. Not surprisingly, I've always been
good for lunch recommendations in my service areas.

On a wider scale, a knowledge of community needs is
an essential element in developing a collection that will
suit its users. Out of the hundreds of thousands of books,
movies, music, etc. that is released every year, it is the
librarians who select what to get for the library. Selection
can be a complicated task (there are many books written
on the topic), but it's a very important one.

2. Library staff have tangible skills

There is a reason that librarians spend a couple of years in graduate school getting an Masters of Library and Information Science (MLIS or MLS) degree—is it to learn how to renew books? It is not. In fact, the trouble with a librarian's tangible skills is that they tend to hide in plain sight: To put it simply, librarians (and experienced library staff) know how to evaluate information and people, joining the two when appropriate. Though it may sound simple, the evaluation of information (whether that information is in the form of a book, website, or archival ephemera) can in incredibly complex, taking into account a diverse, ever-changing set of variables.

Librarians also know how to find relevant information, an essential part of research. Prerequisite to that is a general understanding of an information landscape; the lay of the land, if you will, when it comes to any subject area. For simple queries, Google is easy. For more complicated research requests, it's useful that librarians understand the nuances of information retrieval systems (a search engine is an example of an information retrieval system, there are many others); the general public neither knows nor cares how to structure a search to get the best, most relevant, results. Which is fine, tracking down information is the bailiwick of librarians!

3. Library staff has organizational memory

Just as staff understand their community, long-serving staff members also understand the culture of the organization. They remember when the library tried this or that, and can give invaluable feedback on how to make the initiative work better now. That same experience is also true in charting the many changes that libraries have undergone since their formation. Not just the now-ubiquitous presence of computers, but literacy tutoring (libraries didn't always offer that), trends in collection development, and much more! Though it rarely comes up for the public, as a librarian, I assure you that the historical context provided by experienced staff is seen by me as a welcome insight into the library's world, and the world in general.

4. Library staff show up!

Fifty years ago, you only found librarians in the library. With the times, this has changed; outreach to schools, chambers of commerce, senior centers, prisons, local civic organizations, parks, non-profits, and other neighborhood staples is now the norm for most libraries. Library staff go out to these places not just as emissaries of library service, but also to use their unique tangible skills to assist others where they are. In my article "Library Visits Have Gone Way Over the Last Two Decades. Here's Why..." (see: https://tinyurl.com/LibraryVisitsUp), I talk about how librarians embed themselves in other organizations:

"...Some libraries have [formed]

partnerships with nearby non-profits allowing their librarians to temporarily work in those organizations, using their skills in information architecture, metadata development, and (more often than not) technology, to assist in ways that furthers the mission of both the library and the [other party]."

5. Library staff is there to help

Short of the hospital, the purpose of most of the places we go to on a daily basis is to sell us something. At the library, on the other hand, staff's sole purpose is to help! What a refreshing thought, a place you can go where you won't be pressured to purchase, up-sold, or hassled to part with your money. If you need assistance, you can simply ask and you shall receive!

Librarians are specifically trained to ascertain people's needs. When a patron is having trouble formulating a question or explaining what they're looking for, librarians use their reference interview skills to suss out exactly what's needed. And some people may not be aware: It doesn't have to be about books! Though library staff can definitely give book recommendations ("readers advisory" is a library school course), they can help with a plethora of other inquiries.

Studies show that up to 60% of people have experienced "library anxiety". If you're one of those people, don't be afraid. Library staff is there to help!

There you have it, five reasons why library staff is

crucial to communities. Though it doesn't have to stop at five! Obviously, every library lover knows that there are many more reasons why library staff are the cat's meow. Truly, I'd bet that somewhere in the world at this very moment, a library staff member is making someone's day. It's a truth that makes me smile!

STORYTIME

Like the chapter on "Helping Students," storytime is such an integral part of service at public libraries that it's easy to forget about all of the crucial educational benefits such as motor coordination, literacy, and social skills it can provide – for the kids, of course, but also for the adults in the room.

A SWEET REVIEW

I present a monthly evening bedtime program for families called "Pajama-Rama." I intentionally choose stories and songs to create a mood of cozy togetherness, so that by the end everyone feels wrapped in a blanket of soft words and songs.

During one program, I noticed an older gentleman sitting at the back of the room by himself. He didn't interact with anyone there, and he left as soon as the program was over. The following month he was back, sitting alone by the door. He stayed for the whole program, and left immediately when it ended.

The next day he approached me while I was standing behind the information desk. He said, "You're the one who does the program for children, yes? You play the instrument and read aloud?" I said, yes, that's me. He leaned into the desk and said, "You know, I was an orphan growing up, and no one ever read stories to me. Watching you sing and read to them, I realized what I missed. You are a gift."

Margaret Miles
Fairfax, CA

JUDGMENT-FREE ZONE

While working in the public library I began to notice a family in the library whom I had not seen before. Each week they would wheel in their newborn twins and browse the DVD aisles—a tell-tale sign of new parenthood and the brutal hours kept due to feedings. I worked behind the circulation desk and so would chat with them while they were checking out their materials and, even though they were generally asleep the whole time, gush over how sweet their new additions were. A new mom myself, I understood the experience and how life-changing the event truly is, but I also understood how ostracizing and exhausting it can be.

Noting the slumped shoulders, bags under the eyes, and robotic moves made to get through the library in order to find some movies, I began to tell them about our wonderful story time for children ages 0-24 months. At first they were dubious that this was for them, but each week they returned and asked me another question about story time: Was it noisy? Is it okay if the kids cry? What if you need to leave the room? Are there other babies?, etc. I listened to their questions and understood their concerns: The underlying questions surrounded the fear of being judged. I leaned over the desk closer to them, looked at their tired, drawn faces, and said "This is a judgment-free zone. You can make noise. The babies can cry. You can walk in and out and story time as you need.

It's a great place to meet other parents who are in the same boat as you. And we will never judge you".

The physical signs of stress diminished momentarily and sheer gratitude (mixed with exhaustion) took over as they simultaneously said two loaded words: "Thank you."

Jen Park
Mahwah, NJ

THE VALUE OF STORYTIME

As a Youth Librarian, one of my most powerful memories is of working with an agency that supported teen parents, helping them learn life skills to enable them to stay in school, as well as to be better parents and manage the added stresses babies bring.

I met with the teen parent group regularly to do fun, interactive baby storytimes, modeling ways to interact with their babies that would help with brain development as well as sharing information about early literacy and language acquisition.

After one storytime where I'd talked about the importance of repetition, the value of singing and reading and talking with babies, and the benefits of snuggling and cuddling on growing brains, a 17-year old teen father talked with me about how his interactions with his son had changed since participating in the storytimes.

Initially, he'd not talked to his baby very much because the baby didn't talk back. He didn't understand that babies develop speech and language skills by hearing adults talk, sing, and read with them, and that realization blew his mind. He started being more intentional about talking directly to the baby and when he noticed the baby's responsiveness, the smiling, the eye contact, the body wiggling, it helped him understand that he was teaching his baby how to communicate!

The realization of how important his actions were in his child's life was eye-opening for him, and the library was a huge part of that life-changing process.

Natasha Forrester Campbell
Portland, OR

ACKNOWLEDGMENTS

There are so many people that made this book possible, directly and indirectly. Considering the former first, I would like to express my gratitude to the contributors to this volume – without your willingness to turn your life experiences into impact stories, we would have no book. Likewise, a big thank you goes to Yago Cura for being in the right place at the right time to invigorate me to take this project off the shelf and give it the final push to make it into a book. That last bit would not have been possible without the work of artist/designer extraordinaire, Autumn Anglin (@greygirlgraphics), who made numerous original paintings, used her keen aesthetic sense, and exhibited heroic patience in making this such a beautiful book.

Needless to say, this book is an indirect result of nearly twenty years of library work as a teen volunteer, then Messenger Clerk, with Los Angeles Public Library (LAPL), a student at the University of California, Los Angeles (UCLA) School of Education & Information Studies, an intern with Moorpark City Library, and various roles with LA County Library. A great many people have been generous with me during this time, but I will always especially treasure the beginning of my library life at the Will & Ariel Durant Library. Hannah Kramer, Al Rice, Wendy Horowitz, Hillary Perelyubskiy (nee George), Hillary St. George, Jane Dobija, Ro

Gendrett, Lupo Calaycay, Boris Korinman, Mary Mar, Daniel Balian, Margarita Shvarts, and Yelena Pevsner, thank you for teaching me how to be a librarian.

Thank you also to all of the patrons I have had the pleasure of serving and collaborating with, and who have become my friends. There's no way I can list all of you here, so I won't try. Please know that I have left a little of my heart in Lancaster (CA), West Hollywood, and Topanga.

Thank you to John Chrastka and Patrick "PC" Sweeney of EveryLibrary for trusting me to write and edit under your banner. Founding the *EveryLibrary Medium Magazine* made me a more confident and capable writer and editor.

Finally, the biggest gratitude belongs to my family: My parents, Augustina Kapnik and Vladimir Kagan, who showed me how to be a person. My twin brother, Igor Kagan, for his humor and for being a person who fights for a more just world. And thank you to my wife, Ashley Kagan, who inspires me every day with her goodness. Thank you for believing in me!

APPENDIX A – RECIPE CARD FOR A LIBRARY IMPACT STORY

Library Impact Story (serves thousands)

Ingredients:
- Choose two of the following:
  - Protagonist (single person or group)
  - Situation
  - Time
  - Setting
- One event, or series of similar events (make sure it is library-related)
- One concluding statement

Directions:

1) Open the story by setting the scene wth your choice of two openers. Keep it brief.

2) Add the event and describe until it is clear what happened.

3) Once the event is clearly described, sprinkle in your concluding statement. At this point, the impact of your event should be obvious. If it is not, go back to step two and describe your event differently, or if all else fails, choose a different event.

APPENDIX B – WHAT'S NEXT?

Libraries in the United States receive over a billion visits every year, so there are obviously a lot of library users out there. Why, then, are we constantly reading about libraries fighting for their very survival? The answer, in my opinion, is that most library users do not understand that without their active support, there may eventually be no libraries left to visit. Consequently, here are five simple ways to make sure that trouble and your library never meet:

1. Visit Regularly

The easiest one is what most library supporters already do. It is the reason libraries have over a billion visits and circulate double that amount of items every year. That said, if you haven't been to the library in a while, do drop in. Libraries are always adding surprising new services. Why not try something different? Attend a lecture, concert, or workshop, spend a quiet afternoon perusing magazines, take your work off-site for a day (libraries are ideal places to work). There's so much you can do at the library!

2. Join the Friends of the Library or the Foundation

Most libraries have support organizations whose mission is to raise money directly benefiting the library. Friends of the Library groups are typically the most active, local proponents of the library—traditionally, they host booksales, run a small gift shop, or organize mixers. Joining or donating to a Friends group is usually very low-key and requires little in terms of time commitment (they'll be happy with whatever you can do or give). But the results are tremendous! Many libraries are able to pay for programming solely due to the support of their Friends group.

Foundations are more hands-off groups—they also raise money, but do so on a grander scale to fund large projects. While a Friends group may fund a $250 program, a Library Foundation would be more likely to work on a $15,000 computer upgrade or the creation of a Small Business Center (complete with potential naming rights). Consequently, if you are a successful business owner with little time on your hands but a desire to serve the community, working with a Library Foundation would be the way to go. They are well-equipped to handle large monetary or in-kind donations, and can advise about other sponsorship opportunities.

3. Send a Letter to Your Elected Officials

Here's a 30-minute way to make a monumental difference: Send a letter to your elected officials extolling the life-changing influence of your library. It doesn't have to be long or complex; a few paragraphs and your signature are just right. Why is this vital? Because many elected officials may not have the time or interest to learn how outstanding their libraries are. So when budget time comes around, they have little evidence with which to weigh library funding. A yearly letter from an actual constituent reminding them that libraries are a smart investment is a lot more persuasive than library staff reports, even if both say the same thing.

Want to go a step further? Organize a letter-writing tea party! It's easy: Invite a few local library lovers, give them stamps, envelopes, pen and paper, and put on the kettle!

4. Support EveryLibrary

While it's true that most tax-supported municipal public libraries are funded locally, that is far from the end of the story when it comes to keeping libraries going. EveryLibrary is the only national organization that rallies people around libraries. Friends groups, Foundations, and the American Library Association (ALA) are severely limited in the political arena due to their tax status. Not EveryLibrary, which is a 501(c)4. Simply put: What the NRA is for gun folks, EveryLibrary is for libraries.

So what exactly does EveryLibrary do? First of all, EveryLibrary provides training and support to any library in the United States that has a referendum or measure on the ballot and asks for assistance. Second, they raise public awareness about the important roles libraries play in people's lives. Third, they help bring justice for libraries and librarians by leading mail-in and other direct action campaigns.

I am an advisor to EveryLibrary and Contributing Editor to the *EveryLibrary Medium Magazine*. I volunteer my time at these roles because I believe in EveryLibrary's mission and feel that their work is important.

5. Spread the Word

The final way you can help libraries stay around forever is simply by spreading the word about how awesome they are! When you see a library article in the media, share it on your feeds and tell your friends about it. If your local library has a social media presence, follow them, share their successes, and interact with their posts! And when you see nay-sayers poo-pooing libraries, put them in their place (this handy guide can help: https://tinyurl.com/SnappyLibraryFAQs).

One of the biggest challenges for libraries is getting the word out about their many services. While big companies have multi-million dollar marketing budgets, libraries do the best they can stretching every cent to serve the public. So lend a hand and spread the word!

These five steps aren't the only things you can do to keep libraries around forever, but they're a quick and excellent start at actively supporting the institution you love!

Editor's Bio

Oleg Kagan is an author, editor, speaker, writing coach and, of course, librarian. He has had his writing published on sites all over the web, as well as numerous literary journals and anthologies. He founded, and serves as a Contributing Editor, for the *EveryLibrary Medium Magazine* where his articles have received over 200,000 views. As a speaker, Mr. Kagan has presented widely on literary and library-related topics to audiences of up to several thousand people. He has worked at libraries in the greater Los Angeles area for the past two decades, currently coordinating community engagement for one of the largest library systems in the United States. He is on the Advisory Board of EveryLibrary (where he is a media advisor), and the creative consultancy Catalyst Muse. He lives in west Los Angeles with his wife, Ashley (also a librarian), and toddler, Michael.

Other Books by HINCHAS Press

Ghazals for Foley
Edited by Yago Cura (2016)
ISBN: 978-0-9845398-7-1

Librarians with Spines, Vol. 01
Edited by Max Macias and Yago Cura (2017)
ISBN: 978-0-9845398-8-8

Librarians with Spines, Vol. 02
Edited by Max Macias and Yago Cura (2018)
ISBN: 978-1-7324848-2-5

Whispering to God and the City
by Jesus Cortez (2018)
ISBN: 978-0-9845398-9-5

Coming Soon

Librarians with Spines, Vol. 03
Edited by Max Macias and Yago Cura

8 LA Poets
Edited by Linda Ravenswood

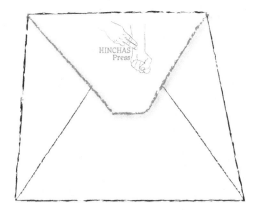

HICHAS Press now offers tiered zine subscription plans.

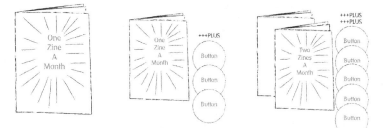

HINCHAS Press is a Los Angeles-based micropress that publishes zines, poetry, poetry in translation, and library science non-fiction. HINCHAS supports social justice initiatives, and advocates for bilingual literacy endeavors, especially along portions of the Américas that are monolingual.

www.hinchaspress.com

Instagram @hinchas_press

Made in the USA
Columbia, SC
01 April 2021